A Trip to the FIRE STATION

Jeffrey A. Rucker

Rosen Classroom Books & Materials™
New York

A fire station is where **firefighters** stay when they are not fighting fires.

Many fire stations have two floors. The bottom floor is where the fire trucks are parked.

The top floor is where firefighters stay when they are on duty. They can slide down a pole to get to the fire truck quickly.

Many firefighters work for twenty-four hours in a row. They eat and sleep at the station when they are on duty.

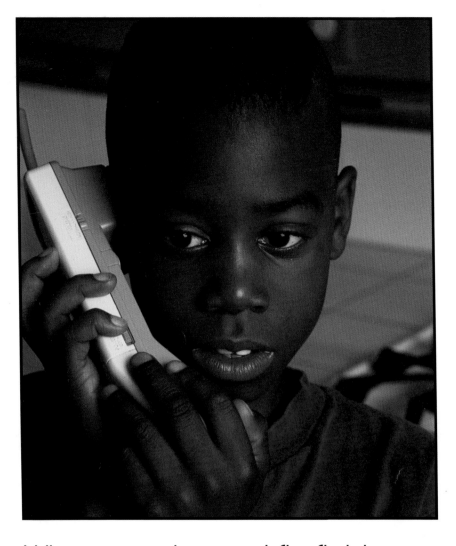

When people need firefighters
to put out a fire, they call **911**.
You can call this number to get
help fast.

The person who answers your call will tell the firefighters where the fire is.

The firefighters must wear heavy **gear** to fight the fire. This gear keeps them safe from the fire.

Firefighters use **hoses** to **spray** water on the fire. Water helps the firefighters put out the fire.

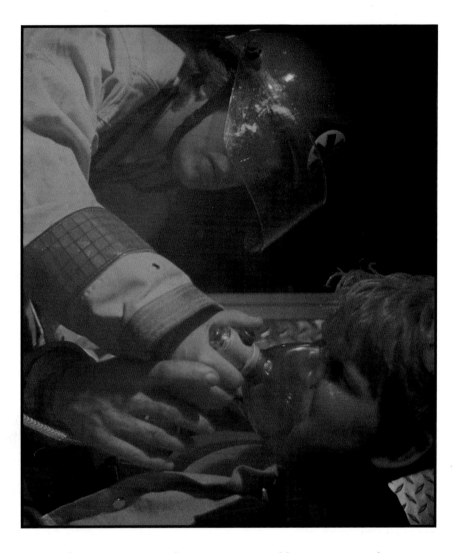

Firefighters do more than put out fires. Firefighters must also know **first aid** to help someone who is hurt.

Firefighters also teach children about fire safety. Children must be careful around fire to keep themselves safe.

GLOSSARY

firefighter A person who puts out fires.

first aid Care given to a person who is sick or hurt.

gear Clothes or tools needed to do a job.

hose A tool used to put water on fire.

911 The phone number that is used to get help quickly.

spray To put a stream of water on something.